Embrace the Pun!

PANEL CARTOONS BY BARRY CORBETT

Embrace the Pun

Published by
Corbett Design Associates
2 Courthouse Lane, Suite 14F
Chelmsford, MA 01824

International Standard (ISBN) # 0-9762294-2-0
Library of Congress Control Number: 2005907402

Printed in the USA

First Printing, 2005

In Memory of Kap.

Special thanks to Jim Corbett, Kathy Corbett and Brian Codagnone for gag writing assistance.

In the Beginning

My partner Brian Codagnone and I joined forces in 2000 and set up our cartooning website, corbettfeatures.com. We knew that we had some solid comic features and planned to self syndicate directly to the newspaper industry. Brian had already been publishing his popular comic strip *Misfits*, and I had just finished developing my first strip, *Rafferty*. We felt that the web would be a great marketing tool to introduce our newest concepts and give us some national exposure.

It has been a valuable experience, exposing our creations to a worldwide audience. In time we introduced *Star Crossed, S1019, Ginger & Shadow* and *Emotional Chaos*. We've been in contact with fellow cartoonists all over the world and eventually were offered a contract with Color Chips India, Ltd to syndicate our features throughout Southeast Asia. Many of the cartoons found in *Embrace the Pun* were developed for our weekly caption writing contest, *Writer's Block*. I hope you enjoy the cartoons and find some time to catch up with the rest of our work at corbettfeatures.com.

Pun (pun) *n.*   the humorous use of a word, or of words which are formed or sounded alike but have different meanings, in such a way as to play on two or more of the possible applications; a play on words. — *vi.* ***punned, pun'ning*** to make puns

Synonyms: ambiguity, calembour, conceit, double entendre, double meaning, equivoque, joke, paronomasia, quibble, quip, witticism, amphibiology, equivocation, innuendo, joke

"Puns may be the lowest form of wit and therefore the foundation of all wit."

— Henry Erskine

"Hanging is too good for a man who makes puns; he should be drawn and quoted."

— Fred Allen

"The goodness of the true pun is in direct ratio to its intolerability."

— Edgar Allen Poe

"It is a form of wit, to which wise men stoop and fools aspire."

— Ambrose Bierce

"The pun is a pistol let off at the ear; not a feather to tickle the intellect."

— Charles Lamb

"A pun is the lowest form of humor —if you didn't think of it first."

— Oscar Levant

Alice finds herself face to face with a charging rhino.

Long Johns Silver.

"I see that attendance continues to be an issue."

Try as he might, Lloyd could never get past the Caller I.Q.

Kevorkian was confident of victory.
After all, Heimlich only had the one maneuver.

"If I had your looks, I'd go into modeling."

"It's called 'The Outdoors'.
I'm broadcasting it over the Internet."

Wanda didn't get to be the top fairy by
waiting around for things to happpen.

4

"This one really speaks to me."

"Oh, yeah...where's Mr. Optimist now?"

"In Recovery!! Nuts! This thing's running slow again."

"He's very smart. You just need to work on his focus."

Long after the grammar school years, Brenda fights
her compulsion to hoard toilet paper rolls.

"Sorry, buddy. You're in tomorrow's cartoon."

The Law Firm of Lemming, Lemming, Lemming, Lemming, Lemming, Lemming....

"Do you ever wonder who you were in a previous life?"

Cowboy Bart is quite at home on the range.

"I should have name YOU Cheetah."

In his younger days Spock was quite the comedian.

Tex encounters the Knick-Knack Indians.

*"I understand you'se has asked to be removed
from our mailing list."*

"Honey, slap on some of this and they'll be drawn to you like... well, you know."

"The first thing we need to work on is your fear of getting on the couch."

12

Great Birds of Praise.

"40 Days!! Rats!! Re-start!"

"A simple plot device should do it. By the way, have you heard of our 3-Sequel Maintenance Plan?"

"I come from a long line of horse thieves."

Conspiracy theorists surmise that Lincoln may have survived.

Stipple-Man vs. the Cross-Hatch Crusader.

Once a year, Edward catches up with cousins
Rock & Paper-Hands.

"I'm very disappointed in you, Rusty. We were
just starting to make some progress here."

16

DUMB AND DAHMER

PYREX of the CARIBBEAN

"You're just dying for me to say it, aren't you?"

"Jenkins, you fool!! You've compressed the trash down into a singularity!!"

"You will be visited by 39 ghosts.
We've updated our holiday list again."

"Miss Jones, cancel my 3 O'clock and get my
attorney on the line."

Doctor Scholl and Mr. Hyde.

"Yeah, it's great, but these roaming charges are killing me."

"... and the Award for Outstanding Feats
in Levitation..."

Close Encounters of the Third Period.

"Hold on, pal. These are Use-em-or-lose-em minutes."

"Sidewinder!!"

22

"Billy!! You're tracking India Ink all over the rug."

Concept by Jim Corbett

Heart Attack: Worst Case Scenario.

23

Sometimes Edna is her own worst enemy.

Chuck is no longer just a face in the crowd with his New Holographic Heckler.

The ill-advised Etch-N-Sketch Museum at San Andreas.

*"I'll give you 'Regular Joe' #1
for that 'Desk Bound Paper Pusher' #14."*

25

America's new Under-Class.

"Louis wants the money you owe him...
or do I have to call the boys over?"

"One Early Bird Special."

"It just doesn't have the same panache."

"While you're at it, Houdini... see if you can find the last 12 years of my life in there."

Magnus was not one to volunteer for the away missions after the unfortunate incident in the Sol System.

"Of course I'm self-absorbed. I'm a sponge!!"

Little Vinnie was not enamored of homework on the weekend.

The Marquis de Shade.

With attendance down, Father Callahan turns to new revenue sources.

Clarence Birdseye's Last Request.

"Oh, I thought you meant figuratively!"

Leonard gains a new appreciation of irony.

"One more time, Mr. Page... Stairway to Heaven!"

*Morale has improved since the addition
of the tanning booth.*

"He looks really ticked off this time, O'Hara!"

"There go the Hendersons.
I'd heard they were splitting up."

Kang the Mighty Conqueror was known forever
after as The Trouser King.

*Years later, The Great Pumpkin would
continue to taunt Linus.*

Hutchins always had to get the last laugh.

"Young Man! You stop feeding your evil twin this instant!"

In the old days, we had to continually feed the screensaver.

"Just once I'd like to see an invasion go smoothly."

Drag Racing... the Sport of Queens.

Captain Chameleon's powers served him well,
long after retirement.

"How's this for long distance service?"

"But honey... he's just not our kind!"

New Demon-O's... a Surprise in Every Box!!

"Ralph, it's the Paper Boy."

Phyllis exercises her demons.

"Maybe I should have picked up that ice cube maker."

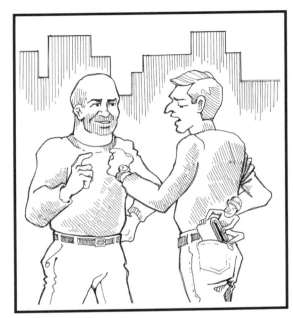

Eddie started out small but soon moved
on to bigger jobs.

Skate Bard.

"You lost points for the poorly drawn weapon."

"Rock, Rock, Rock again. Us never settle anything!"

"I hate these double-headers."

In a rare stroke of genius,
Ernie sells his in-soles to the devil.

44

"Okay, we understand the irony.
Just plug it back in!"

"We're dead meat. They gave us 'The Hanging Judge.'"

People Unclear on the Concept.

"You can forget your tip at table seven."

Genetic Engineering at its Finest.

Casting Call at the Cartoon Cliché Dept.

Concept by Jim Corbett

The Atlantis Braves have yet to turn a double play.

Billy-Joe couldn't believe his luck.
Some durned fool left a 6 pack behind.

*Frederick begins to comprehend the gravity
of his situation.*

Seemed like a good idea at the time.

The Alpine Skater.

The Coin-Op Sumo Wash.

"Well, whatta ya know... it IS in the fine print."

Bears are known to have a grim sense of humor.

Andrew is forced to admit that he's
Pictographically Challenged.

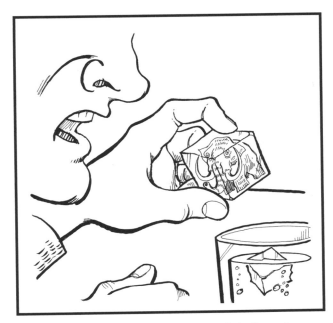

The old "Mammoth in the Ice Cube" gag is
still big at Paleontologist parties.

"If you ask me... hangin's too good for 'em!"

A hush fell over the crowd...
then again, it was Mime Night.

54

Frankie likes to start every day with a blank slate.

Eddie's Last Known Performance.

*"Jonathan. He's not eating his green beans!
Get the Kryptonite!"*

Nobody drags out an at-bat like Kowalski.

"They appear to have worshipped this strange, silver God."

Flash uses up his last exposure.

"If she thinks I'm just gonna come running on home, wagging my tail behind me..."

Packing Peanuts.

Sports Cartoons

Every now and then I make a brief foray into the sporting news. These cartoons were published in early 2005, while the NHL and their player's union were at each other's throats over the issue of a salary cap.

Baseball

In 2003 our beloved Boston Red Sox and New York Yankees (a.k.a. The Evil Empire) met once again in the American League Championship Series. Things actually looked good for the local nine until the 8th inning of Game 7. Once again, the Bambino invoked his legendary curse, and we went down to a crushing defeat. Much was written about the effectiveness of Pedro Martinez after reaching the 100 pitch count. It proved to be a factor, as Grady Little left him in to start the eighth.

Redemption

Alas, 86 years without a championship! Then, the unthinkable happened. In 2004 the Sox and Yanks squared off again in the ALCS and the Red Sox quickly found themselves down 0–3. Led by fan favorites "Big Papi" Ortiz, Curt Schilling and Johnny Damon, they literally rose from the dead, charging back to take the Series—the greatest comeback in the history of baseball. They didn't stop there, winning 8 straight games on their way to the World Series Championship!

"Sorry, but I'm just too busy to deal with layoffs."

The sign did say "Food and Spirits".

The cold, lonely life of the popsicle farmer.

"Okay, now he's just showing off."

Death comes unexpectedly, but with impeccable manners.

For a minute there, Malcom almost had an idea.

"Settle down, pardner. Tain't nothin' but Fool's Gold."

"Oh, for heaven's sake, Martin. Use the spray!!"

"No man is an island, Benson. For God's sake,
it's right there in the company handbook."

"Twelve items or less, honey. You think we're kidding?"

"Ouch! Somebody sure got up on the
wrong side of bed this morning!"

"Here's your problem, Mac.
You've got another goalie stuck in the Hyper Drive."

"Remember me...Gandalf the Grey? Thanks to new,
improved TidyBrite I'm Gandalf the Dazzling White!"

"That's quite a beautiful flower bed, Mrs. Brown.
If you buy some cookies, it stays that way."

"*Young Man ! You turn the gravity back on this instant !!*"

"Walter, the boys and I think you're enjoying this sheepskin thing a little too much."

"Can somebody please explain the concept of Team-Building to Raymond?"

70

"Anchormen who work too much and the women who leave them — Tonight on News Center 5!"

"Oh, sorry. I was looking for Gates."

71

"I know it's a cliché but I'm sticking with bipolar."

The "Rolling-in-at-4AM Bird" beats the Early Bird to the worm.

George lingers at Death's door.

"I see circus people. They're everywhere."

Infamous First Drafts:
Alice Down the Laundry Chute

Things were never the same for Spike
once they brought in The Substitute 360 Model.

"Fred, I'm leaving you for Kevin. I just can't be with
a man who has no ambition."

"Now, which one of these guys hit you with the pie?"

Gilligan's recurring nightmare—
Mrs. Howell was the lone survivor.

"This Gates guy is a great client.
He upgrades every year!"

76

The 15th Toon

Back in 2000, one of the cartoonists at Webcomics.com came up with an interesting concept. What would happen if we all tried to come up with a cartoon on the same theme? And so began the 15th Toon. Three criteria would be posted every month, and contributing web cartoonists would upload their solutions on the same day. The results were varied... and somewhat bizarre.

Person: Cowboy
Place: Rodeo
Thing: Roller Skates

Person: Super Hero
Place: Gas Station
Thing: Lobster

Barnum & Bucky's 3-Ring Rodeo proved disastrous.

*In desperation, Lobster Man hurls
the mens room key at Doctor Octane!*

"You're not quite the world beater I thought I'd married."

"Hey, whadda ya say we go find us a China Shop?"

"Hey... wait a minute!
We don't have a unisex rest room!"

Product placement hits the classics.

"At around 8:15 there'll be a fender-bender on Broadway, and you'll want to avoid Rte. 95 before 10:20."

"Yup, looks like a Mime Field, boys."

"Yes, my client did put her in a pumpkin shell...
but remember, he kept her very well."

The Ultimate Specialist.

81

Rusty encounters the Elite Postal Revenge Squad.

"The Bills!! The Bills!!"

Oogie was tough, but not one of the brighter goons.

The Saga of Alien Gonzalez.

"Stop complaining. We had to do something improve our image."

84

"Eegor! Stop playing with your food!"

Great Failures in Mascot Design:
The Bipolar Bear.

"Will you knock it off...we're trying to concentrate!"

Thursday is KareYokum Night.

Kung Flu Fighting.

"Okay. Here's where you little dogies learn to git along."

"Tough split there, Eddie."

Some Favorite Webcomics

Check out some of these hidden gems. Most of these talented artists publish daily, and in full color. They're all free, and unlike traditional newspaper comics, you can interact with them through web blogs and discussion boards.

Screams
by Guy Gilchrist
www.gilchriststudios.com

Misfits
by Brian Codagnone
www.corbettfeatures.com

Innies and Outties
by Leonard M. Cachola
www.inniesandoutties.keenspace.com

Hey Harry!
by Thomas Ebert
www.heyharry.com

Sev Trek
by Australian cartoonist John Cook
www.cartoons.sev.com

Bruno the Bandit
by Ian McDonald
www.brunothebandit.com

Bob the Squirrel
by Frank Page
http://www.bobthesquirrel.com/

Hagen Toons
by Canadian artist Ralph Hagen
www.hagenstoons.com

Mojo Planet
by Paul Zarza
www.mojoplanet.org

Sluggy Freelance
by Pete Abram
www.sluggy.com

A.P.E. Force
by Marcus Shockley & Kirk Siee
www.apeforce.net/afcomic

Kevin & Kell
by Bill Holbrook
www.kevinandkell.com

Happy Glyphs
by John Steventon
www.HappyGlyphs.com

Unlikely Stories
Michael P. Stype
www.members.csinet.net/mpspbs

Big Fat Whale
by local hero Brian McFadden
www.bigfatwhale.com

S1019
by Brian Codagnone
www.corbettfeatures.com

Lost & Found
by Matt Milligan
www.lostandfoundcomic.com

Schlock Mercenary
by Howard Tayler
www.schlockmercenary.com

Scrag Ends
by British cartoonist Brian Hughes
www.btinternet.com/~scragends

Astounding Space Thrills
by Steve Conley
www.astoundingspacethrills.com

PVP
by Scott Kurtz
www.pvponline.com

Cartoon Anthology Sites
www.webcomics.com
www.astronerdboy.com
www.onlinecomics.net
www.thecartoonsite.com
www.stus.com
www.fleen.com
www.humorlinks.com
www.keenspace.com